THE ULTIMATE
LOS ANGELES RAMS
TRIVIA BOOK

A Collection of Amazing Trivia Quizzes
and Fun Facts for Die-Hard Rams Fans!

Ray Walker

Exclusive Free Book
Crazy Sports Stories

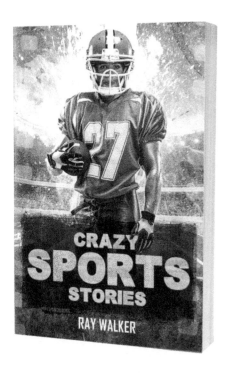

As a thank you for getting a copy of this book I would like to offer you a free copy of my book Crazy Sports Stories which comes packed with interesting stories from your favorite sports such as Football, Hockey, Baseball, Basketball and more.

Grab your free copy over at
RayWalkerMedia.com/Bonus

CONTENTS

INTRODUCTION

Team fandom should be inspirational. Our attachment to our favorite teams should fill us with pride, excitement, loyalty, and a sense of fulfillment in knowing that we are part of a community with many other fans who feel the same way.

Rams fans are no exception. With a rich, successful history in the NFL, the Rams have inspired their supporters to strive for greatness with their tradition of colorful players, memorable eras, big moves, and unique moments.

This book is meant to be a celebration of those moments, and an examination of the collection of interesting, impressive, or important details that allow us to understand the full stories behind the players and the team.

You may use the book as you wish. Each chapter contains 20 quiz questions in a mixture of multiple-choice and true-false formats, an answer key (Don't worry, it's on a separate page!), and a section of 10 "Did You Know?" factoids about the team.

Some will use it to test themselves with the quiz questions. How much Rams history did you really know? How many of the finer points can you remember? Some will use it competitively (Isn't that the heart of sports?), waging contests with friends and fellow devotees to see who can lay claim to being the biggest fan. Some will enjoy it as a learning experience, gaining insight to enrich their fandom and add color to their understanding of their favorite team. Still others may use it to teach, sharing the wonderful anecdotes inside to inspire a new generation of fans to hop aboard the Rams bandwagon.

Whatever your purpose may be, we hope you enjoy delving into the amazing background of Los Angeles Rams football!

Two quick geographical notes are important to keep in mind. One: The Rams franchise has moved between cities multiple times. For the sake of consistency, the franchise is referred to as "Los Angeles" throughout this book, but all questions include data from the team's history as a whole, even the years when they were not based in Los Angeles. Two: Other professional teams have also played in Los Angeles, but this book is focused on the Rams. Questions that ask about "Los Angeles" do not include data from the L.A. Raiders, L.A. Chargers, etc.

Oh, and for the record, information and statistics in this book are current up to the beginning of 2021. The Rams will surely topple more records and win more awards as the seasons pass, so keep this in mind when you're watching the next game with your friends, and someone starts a conversation with "Did you know...?" to share some trivia.

CHAPTER 1:

ORIGINS & HISTORY

QUIZ TIME!

1. In which year did the Rams begin playing in the National Football League?

   a. 1937
   b. 1941
   c. 1946
   d. 1950

2. The franchise was nearly called the Cleveland Guardians, partially because of some of the famous statue forms on a local bridge called the Guardians and partially to honor a defunct rugby team from the city by that name.

   a. True
   b. False

3. How was the nickname "Rams" chosen for the team?

   a. Majority owner Homer Marshman chose the name after being inspired by seeing a majestic herd of rams on a mountainside.

b. "Rams" was the winner chosen in a local newspaper contest held to generate naming ideas for the franchise.

c. It was selected by general manager Damon Wetzel, who greatly admired the Fordham University Rams in the NCAA.

d. Owner Dan Reeves, who had made his fortune with the Dodge Automobile Company, thought that it tied in nicely with the Dodge Ram truck series.

4. In which season did the Rams begin to play at the new SoFi Stadium?

    a. 2006
    b. 2010
    c. 2018
    d. 2020

5. Who founded the Los Angeles Rams?

    a. Paul Brown
    b. Homer Marshman and Damon Wetzel
    c. George Steinbrenner
    d. Dan Reeves and Fred Levy Jr.

6. In which season did the Rams earn their first-ever playoff berth?

    a. 1938
    b. 1941
    c. 1945
    d. 1953

7. The Los Angeles Rams won more games than any other NFL team during the period between 1995 and 2005.

a. True

b. False

8. How many times in their franchise history have the Rams won a division title?

   a. 8
   b. 13
   c. 17
   d. 26

9. Who were the first two Rams players ever to be named to the NFL All-Pro Team when they were Second Team selections?

   a. Quarterback Parker Hall and guard Riley Matheson
   b. Halfbacks Jim Gilette and Fred Gehrke
   c. Center Chuck Cherundolo and fullback Johnny Drake
   d. End Steve Pritko and tackle Eberle Schultz

10. Where do the Los Angeles Rams rank among NFL franchises when it comes to most Super Bowl championships won?

    a. 4th overall
    b. Tied for 9th overall
    c. 11th overall
    d. Tied for 15th overall

11. How did the Rams fare during their 50th anniversary season in the NFL?

    a. Missed the playoffs
    b. Lost in the Wild Card playoffs to the Washington Redskins

   c. Lost in the NFC Championship to the Chicago Bears

   d. Lost in the Super Bowl to the Pittsburgh Steelers

12. The longest stretch the Rams have gone without making the playoffs is eleven years, from 1956 to 1966.

   a. True

   b. False

13. Which team did the Rams face in their first-ever NFL game on September 10, 1937?

   a. Philadelphia Eagles

   b. Chicago Cardinals

   c. Detroit Lions

   d. Green Bay Packers

14. What were the details surrounding the Rams' first-ever shutout in the NFL?

   a. It was a 28-0 loss to the Detroit Lions in 1937.

   b. It was a 10-0 win over the Chicago Bears in 1938.

   c. It was a 6-0 loss to the Brooklyn Dodgers in 1938.

   d. It was a 21-0 win over the Green Bay Packers in 1939.

15. Which player kicked the first-ever field goal for the Rams?

   a. Harry Matos

   b. Bob Snyder

   c. Johnny Drake

   d. Ed Goddard

16. As of 2021, the Los Angeles Rams are tied with the Green Bay Packers and the Minnesota Vikings as the franchises

that have sent more players to the Pro Bowl than any other NFL franchise.

a. True
b. False

17. How did the Rams fare in their first-ever NFL playoff run after moving to Los Angeles?

a. Lost in the conference playoff to the Detroit Lions
b. Lost in the NFL Championship to the Cleveland Browns
c. Won in the NFL Championship over the Cleveland Browns
d. Lost in the NFL Championship to the Philadelphia Eagles

18. What is the Los Angeles franchise record for most victories recorded by the club in a single regular season?

a. 11
b. 12
c. 13
d. 14

19. What is the name of the Rams' team mascot?

a. Rampage
b. Randy the Ram
c. Bull
d. The Rams do not have a team mascot.

20. The Los Angeles football franchise has, at some point, been included in the Western Conference, the Western

Division, the National Conference, and the Coastal Division within the NFL.

a. True
b. False

QUIZ ANSWERS

1. A – 1937

2. B – False

3. C – It was selected by general manager Damon Wetzel, who greatly admired the Fordham University Rams in the NCAA.

4. D – 2020

5. B – Homer Marshman and Damon Wetzel

6. C – 1945

7. B – False

8. C – 17

9. C – Center Chuck Cherundolo and fullback Johnny Drake

10. D – Tied for 15th overall

11. B – Lost in the Wild Card playoffs to the Washington Redskins

12. B – False

13. C – Detroit Lions

14. A – It was a 28-0 loss to the Detroit Lions in 1937.

15. B – Bob Snyder

16. B – False

17. D – Lost in the NFL Championship to the Philadelphia Eagles

18. D – 14

19. A – Rampage

20. A – True

DID YOU KNOW?

1. The Rams have played home games at an astounding eight stadiums; almost one per decade. They have been located at three in Ohio, three in California, and two in Missouri.

2. Los Angeles was home to two professional football teams when the Rams arrived in 1946, as the Los Angeles Dons began playing in the All-America Football Conference that same year.

3. SoFi Stadium, the current home of the Rams, is actually located in Inglewood, California. Because Los Angeles is large enough to support two NFL teams, the stadium is also the home of the Los Angeles Chargers as well. Although it just opened in 2020, it has already cycled through two other names: City of Champions Stadium and Los Angeles Stadium at Hollywood Park.

4. While the Rams are an anchor tenant of SoFi Stadium, it is not used exclusively for NFL games. It is home to the NCAA's LA Bowl and is already scheduled to host the College Football Playoff National Championship Game, WrestleMania 39, and some of the events for the 2028 Summer Olympics.

5. No NFL franchise has relocated more often than the Rams. They moved far enough to change the team's name three times: from Cleveland to Los Angeles in 1946, Los Angeles to St. Louis in 1995, and then St. Louis to Los

Angeles in 2016. This doesn't even include relocations within California to Anaheim and Inglewood, during which they maintained "Los Angeles" within the team's name.

6. The first NFL touchdown in Rams history was scored by Johnny Drake. Drake caught a 38-yard pass from Bob Snyder to put the Rams up 7-0 against the Philadelphia Eagles on September 21, 1937.

7. Los Angeles's biggest NFL rival is generally thought to be the San Francisco 49ers, as the two teams battle within the same state and the same division. The 49ers have a slight advantage in the head-to-head rivalry, with five more regular-season wins in the series and a 1-0 playoff record against the Rams.

8. Los Angeles's franchise record for fewest victories recorded by the club in a single, regular season is one, which they have done three times: 1937, 1962, and 2009.

9. Unlike some NFL teams, the Rams employ both male and female cheerleaders to support the squad. Membership does skew heavily female, but the current version of the group includes four males.

10. In the beginning, the Rams struggled. During their first eight years in the NFL, the team did not post a winning record, let alone make the playoffs. But in 1945, new coach Adam Walsh was brought in, and he led the team to a 9-1 record and an NFL Championship, which would be their only title before leaving Cleveland.

CHAPTER 2:

JERSEYS & NUMBERS

QUIZ TIME!

1. When they began playing in the NFL in 1937, the Rams used what color scheme for their home and away uniforms?

    a. Gold and blue

    b. Red and black

    c. Blue, beige, and yellow

    d. White, gold, and black

2. The numbers 0 and 00 have been banned from circulation by Los Angeles ownership, as they are seen to represent a losing attitude.

    a. True

    b. False

3. How many stripes run from the crown to the back of the neck on the current version of the Rams' helmets?

    a. 0

    b. 1

c. 2

d. 3

4. Two excellent Los Angeles Rams each wore number 29 for over five years with the team. Who were these two players?

   a. Running backs Lawrence McCutcheon and Todd Gurley

   b. Linebacker Jack Pardee and safety Adam Archuleta

   c. Running back Marshall Faulk and defensive back Pat Thomas

   d. Running back Eric Dickerson and wide receiver Harold Jackson

5. In which year was approval received for player names to appear on the backs of Rams jerseys?

   a. 1960

   b. 1965

   c. 1970

   d. 1975

6. Which Rams player proved to be most popular with Rams fans in 2020, having sold the most Los Angeles player merchandise on NFL.com?

   a. Defensive tackle Aaron Donald

   b. Quarterback Jared Goff

   c. Wide receiver Robert Woods

   d. Running back Todd Gurley

7. The white jerseys worn by Los Angeles are often said to have been "jinxed," and therefore, the team avoids

wearing them during the Super Bowl whenever the choice is theirs.

   a. True

   b. False

8. Who is the player to wear the highest numbered jersey (number 99) for the most games in Rams franchise history?

   a. Defensive tackle Aaron Donald

   b. Defensive tackle Alvin Wright

   c. Defensive end Grant Wistrom

   d. Defensive end James Hall

9. The current version of the Rams uniform includes two colors. Which of the following are the technical names of the colors used in this scheme?

   a. Navy blue and lemon yellow

   b. Surf blue and sunshine

   c. Rams royal and sol

   d. Rams blue and L.A. gold

10. Three different publications, including *Sports Illustrated*, have named which of the following Los Angeles Rams as the best athlete ever to wear his number in any sport?

   a. Defensive end Jack Youngblood with number 85

   b. Defensive tackle Aaron Donald with number 99

   c. Running back Marshall Faulk with number 28

   d. Quarterback Kurt Warner with number 13

11. Twenty-one players have worn number 11 for the Rams. Which of these players accounted for the most career touchdowns?

    a. Quarterback Jim Everett
    b. Wide receiver Tavon Austin
    c. Wide receiver Josh Reynolds
    d. Quarterback Norm Van Brocklin

12. Star defensive tackle Merlin Olsen is the only Ram to have ever worn the number 74 on his jersey and will continue to be the only one as his number is now retired.

    a. True
    b. False

13. Why did star running back Steven Jackson choose to wear number 39 on the back of his jersey for St. Louis?

    a. Jackson hoped to retire at 39 from his NFL playing days, as "a young man, but with a long and fruitful career" behind him.
    b. It was worn by Hall of Fame running back Larry Csonka, who was Jackson's favorite player as a child.
    c. Jackson is a religious man, and it represented the number of books contained in the Old Testament of the Bible.
    d. His father, Marcus Jackson, was born in the year 1939.

14. How many jersey numbers have the Los Angeles Rams retired for their former players?

    a. 3
    b. 6

c. 8

d. 12

15. Which player competed for the Rams for just five seasons; the shortest tenure of anyone whose number has been retired by the franchise?

    a. Running back Marshall Faulk

    b. Defensive end Jack Youngblood

    c. Quarterback Bob Waterfield

    d. Running back Eric Dickerson

16. Thirteen players have worn the number 1 for Los Angeles, and every single one of them was a quarterback.

    a. True

    b. False

17. Lucky number 7 has been worn by six Rams players over the years. Which athlete wore it for the longest amount of time?

    a. Quarterback Bob Waterfield

    b. Wide receiver Tavon Austin

    c. Tailback Ken Heineman

    d. Quarterback Jim Everett

18. Who is the most recent Rams player to have his number retired by the club?

    a. Offensive tackle Orlando Pace

    b. Quarterback Kurt Warner

    c. Wide receiver Isaac Bruce

    d. Running back Marshall Faulk

19. Which two numbers did star wide receiver Torry Holt wear on the back of his jersey for the Rams, after switching in the middle of his career?

    a. 18 and 81
    b. 9 and 89
    c. 80 and 85
    d. 81 and 88

20. The Rams have retired more jersey numbers than any other NFL franchise has.

    a. True
    b. False

QUIZ ANSWERS

1. B – Red and black

2. B – False

3. A – 0

4. D – Running back Eric Dickerson and wide receiver Harold Jackson

5. C – 1970

6. A – Defensive tackle Aaron Donald

7. B – False

8. A – Defensive tackle Aaron Donald

9. C – Rams royal and sol

10. A – Defensive end Jack Youngblood with number 85

11. A – Quarterback Jim Everett

12. B – False

13. C – Jackson is a religious man, and it represented the number of books contained in the Old Testament of the Bible.

14. C – 8

15. D – Running back Eric Dickerson

16. B – False

17. A – Quarterback Bob Waterfield

18. C – Wide receiver Isaac Bruce

19. D – 81 and 88

20. B – False

DID YOU KNOW?

1. In 1948, Rams halfback Fred Gehrke, who doubled as an artist in the offseason, decided to paint Rams horns onto the team's leather helmets. Gehrke received approval from ownership and was paid $1 for each helmet he painted. When the Rams eventually took the field, marking the first time a team had ever worn a helmet logo, fans erupted in a standing ovation and a trend was born.

2. Fred Gehrke was an innovator in other ways with the Rams as well. In 1946, Gehrke suffered three broken noses while playing, and so, in 1947, he invented the first football facemask. It was made of aluminum, covered in leather, and affixed to his helmet. However, Gehrke found that it impaired his peripheral vision too much and removed the facemask in 1948.

3. From 1964 until 1973, the Rams removed gold entirely as a color that they wore. Instead, the uniforms used a very simple blue-and-white motif during those years.

4. Rams defensive coordinator and, briefly, interim head coach Jim Haslett was so attached to the number he wore during his playing days (55) as a linebacker, that when he purchased a horse ranch in New York, he decided to call it "Double Nickel" as a tribute to that number.

5. In 1973, a pair of Rams had very unusual uniforms. Defensive end Jack Youngblood and linebacker Jim

21

Youngblood (no relation) had to be differentiated and could not use a first initial since both given names began with a "J." Therefore, each was allowed to have his full name on the back of his jersey, with the given name listed above the surname.

6. The first time the Rams ever wore a patch on their uniforms was in 1945. The patch appeared on their sleeves and was designed to show support for the World War II effort made by the country.

7. Superstition may have scared some Rams away from wearing the number 13. Only 13 players in franchise history have chosen it for themselves; although, quarterback Kurt Warner managed to win an MVP and a Super Bowl MVP while wearing the "unlucky" number.

8. Since 1973, the NFL no longer allows players to wear jersey number 0 or 00. Steve Bagarus did wear 0 for two games with the Rams in 1947, which will make him the only player ever to do so.

9. The highest number ever retired by the Los Angeles Rams is number 85, belonging to defensive end Jack Youngblood.

10. For one year only, in 1949, the Rams switched their colors to red and gold. The reason is unclear, but it is possible that they wanted to align with the locally based USC Trojans of the NCAA.

CHAPTER 3:

CATCHY NICKNAMES

QUIZ TIME!

1. By which nickname are the Rams' fans now most commonly referred to?

    a. "The Rams' Reps"

    b. "L.A. Nation"

    c. "Rams Revellers"

    d. "The Mob Squad"

2. Talented Rams running back Marshall Faulk was often referred to as "The Swiss Army Knife" thanks to his ability to seemingly contribute in any way on the field, whether it was running, catching, or blocking.

    a. True

    b. False

3. The home of the Rams from 1980 to 1994, Anaheim Stadium, was also more commonly known by which popular nickname?

    a. "The Big A"

    b. "The Pearly Gates"

c. "Disneyville"

d. "The Big Sombrero"

4. Because of his speed, Los Angeles cornerback Janoris Jenkins was known by players and fans as which animal?

   a. "The Cheetah"

   b. "The Quarter Horse"

   c. "The Jackrabbit"

   d. "The Peregrine Falcon"

5. Why is current Rams quarterback Devlin Hodges known around the league as "Duck"?

   a. Because of an evasive maneuver he has perfected to duck below opposing pass rushers as they dive to tackle him

   b. Because he went to college at the University of Oregon, whose football team is known as the Ducks

   c. Because he has a tattoo of Scrooge McDuck diving into a pit of gold coins on the bicep of his throwing arm

   d. Because he has won numerous state and world championships as a duck caller

6. Which of the following nicknames was given to Rams running back Elroy Hirsch because of the unorthodox way he looked when running with the ball?

   a. "Duck Feet"

   b. "The Penguin"

   c. "Crazy Legs"

   d. "Road Runner"

7. St. Louis quarterback Kurt Warner was known as "Supermarket Jesus" because the undrafted and highly religious Warner had emerged as an annual MVP candidate and savior for the Rams franchise after being signed to the team from his obscure job bagging food at a grocery store.

    a. True
    b. False

8. Why was Rams quarterback Nick Foles given the nickname "Big Dick Nick" by former teammate Connor Barwin?

    a. Because Barwin was impressed by Foles's performance under pressure during the fourth quarter of a close playoff game.
    b. Because Barwin mentioned Foles in response to an internet question about which football player had the largest genitalia.
    c. Because, according to Barwin, Foles refused to ever pick up the check when members of the team went out to dinner together.
    d. Because Foles was fearless and never hesitated when approaching single women to ask for a date or a phone number.

9. What was Los Angeles kicker Greg Zuerlein also known as thanks to his ability to convert long field goals?

    a. "Greg the Leg"
    b. "The Ram Cannon"

c. "Mr. Automatic"

d. "Long Dizztance"

10. Rams kicker Carlos Huerta went by which one-word nickname that reflected his ability to remain calm under pressure?

   a. "Cucumber"

   b. "Iceman"

   c. "Chilly"

   d. "Steady"

11. Which Rams player was known to fans and teammates by the nickname "Big Game," thanks to his performance in high pressure situations during key college games and the Super Bowl?

   a. Quarterback Kurt Warner

   b. Running back Marshall Faulk

   c. Kicker Jeff Wilkins

   d. Wide receiver Torry Holt

12. After engaging in two memorable fights with his former Los Angeles teammates as a newly traded member of the Detroit Lions, ex-Rams offensive tackle Greg Robinson earned the nickname "The Vengeful Ex."

   a. True

   b. False

13. How did Rams linebacker Jack Reynolds earn the nickname "Hacksaw" during his college days?

a. He used a celebration that mimicked sawing up opposing players after taking them down with a big tackle.

b. Rather than lift weights for training, he chopped and cut firewood so that he could make some money and work out at the same time.

c. His great, great grandfather Asa Reynolds was the original inventor of the tool.

d. He cut a car in half using the tool to vent his frustrations after a 38-0 loss.

14. Most NFL fans knew Rams running back "Cadillac" Williams better by his nickname than his real name, which was actually what?

a. Malcolm

b. Stephen

c. Carnell

d. De'Aaron

15. Due to his mediocre results on the field in comparison to the size of his massive contract, Rams quarterback Sam Bradford was given which derisive nickname by a Yahoo columnist?

a. "Con Man"

b. "Sam the Sham"

c. "The Million Dollar Mistake"

d. "Richie Benchwarmer"

16. Los Angeles linebacker James Laurinaitis was called "Little Animal" by his teammates because his father Joe

had been a professional wrestler who went by the name "Animal" in a tag team group called the Road Warriors.

a. True

b. False

17. Which Rams player was known to fans and teammates by the nicknames "The Human Joystick" for his speed and agility, and "The X Factor" for his celebrations?

a. Wide receiver Az-Zahir Hakim

b. Safety John Johnson III

c. Kick returner Dante Hall

d. Wide receiver Tavon Austin

18. Which unflattering nickname was Rams quarterback Chris Chandler given due to his tendency to suffer injuries?

a. "Crystal Chandelier"

b. "The Glass Elbow"

c. "Captain Breakdown"

d. "Mister Sensitive"

19. Rams defensive lineman Gene Lipscomb was given which of the following nicknames because of his 6'6", 284-pound size?

a. "The Refrigerator"

b. "Big Daddy"

c. "The Punisher"

d. "Brick Wall"

20. St. Louis quarterback Ryan Fitzpatrick was known as "The Amish Rifle" because of his bushy, overgrown beard and strong throwing arm.

a. True
b. False

QUIZ ANSWERS

1. D – "The Mob Squad"

2. B – False

3. A – "The Big A"

4. C – "The Jackrabbit"

5. D – Because he has won numerous state and world championships as a duck caller

6. C – "Crazy Legs"

7. B – False

8. B – Because Barwin mentioned Foles in response to an internet question about which football player had the largest genitalia.

9. A – "Greg the Leg"

10. B – "Iceman"

11. D – Wide receiver Torry Holt

12. B – False

13. D – He cut a car in half using the tool to vent his frustrations after a 38-0 loss.

14. C – Carnell

15. A – "Con Man"

16. A – True

17. C – Kick returner Dante Hall

18. A – "Crystal Chandelier"

19. B – "Big Daddy"

20. A – True

DID YOU KNOW?

1. Rams quarterback Ryan Fitzpatrick was noted for his streaky play and depending on whether the streak was good or bad, he was known as "Fitzmagic" or "Fitztragic."

2. The year after kicker Tom Dempsey left the Rams, the NFL instituted a rule known unofficially as the "Tom Dempsey Rule." Many felt that Dempsey, who had no toes on his kicking foot, got extra distance because of a specially crafted flat-toed shoe he wore. The rule stated that a normal shoe must be worn so that controversy could be avoided.

3. Fordham University, Colorado State University, and the University of Rhode Island all use the nickname "Rams," which means that Los Angeles has selected nine players whose team nickname did not change upon joining the NFL.

4. From 1963 to 1967, the Rams employed a defensive front that was called "the most dominant line in football history" by no less an authority than legendary Chicago Bears linebacker Dick Butkus. Rosey Grier, Deacon Jones, Merlin Olsen, and Lamar Lundy wreaked havoc on the field together, and were collectively known as "The Fearsome Foursome."

5. An NFL rule more widely known by its unofficial nickname, the "Deacon Jones Rule," was named after the

longtime Rams defensive lineman. Jones became a Hall-of-Famer in part due to his use of a powerful head slap delivered to opposing offensive linemen while Jones rushed the quarterback. The rule prevents this technique as it was found to be too violent and likely to cause long-term injury.

6. Rams cornerback Jackie Wallace was always on the minds of opposing wide receivers because he liked to hit hard and often used his helmet as the first point of impact before it was known that this could cause long-lasting brain injuries. Wallace became known as "Headhunter" around the league.

7. During the 1950s, the Rams featured nicknames within nicknames. Their stable of running backs was known as the "Bull Elephant Backfield," and prominently featured players like Lester "Dick" Hoerner, Paul "Tank" Younger, and "Deacon" Dan Towler.

8. Physical Rams running back Jerome Bettis was frequently called "The Bus" because of his large size, tough running style, and ability to carry would-be tacklers for extra yards.

9. One of the most memorable plays in Rams franchise history would become known simply as "The Tackle." It occurred when Tennessee Titans wide receiver Kevin Dyson caught a pass on the final play of Super Bowl XXXIV with the Titans needing to go 10 yards to score a game-tying touchdown to send the contest to overtime.

Dyson ran, dove, and stretched for the goal line while being wrapped up by St. Louis Rams linebacker Mike Jones, who stopped Dyson just a few inches short, clinching the championship for the Rams.

10. During the late 1990s and early 2000s, the St. Louis Rams trotted out a record-breaking offense featuring quarterback Kurt Warner, running back Marshall Faulk, and wide receivers Torry Holt, Isaac Bruce, Ricky Proehl, and Az-Zahir Hakim. Their unstoppable prowess earned them the nickname "The Greatest Show on Turf."

CHAPTER 4:

THE QUARTERBACKS

QUIZ TIME!

1. Which of these Rams quarterbacks has been sacked by opponents by far the most times during the span of their career with the Rams?

    a. Jim Everett
    b. Marc Bulger
    c. Jared Goff
    d. Roman Gabriel

2. Quarterback Kurt Warner holds the top four spots on the Rams' all-time list of most passing touchdowns thrown in a season.

    a. True
    b. False

3. Which quarterback has thrown the most intercepted passes in Los Angeles Rams franchise history, edging out the second-place passer 128-127?

    a. Norm Van Brocklin
    b. Jim Everett

c. Bob Waterfield

d. Vince Ferragamo

4. Who is the Los Angeles Rams' all-time career leader in most passing yards?

   a. Kurt Warner

   b. Sam Bradford

   c. Roman Gabriel

   d. Jim Everett

5. Which Rams player set the franchise record for most passing yards in a season by a Los Angeles quarterback, putting up 4,830?

   a. Kurt Warner

   b. Jared Goff

   c. Marc Bulger

   d. Sam Bradford

6. How many players that have played quarterback for the Rams have been elected to the Pro Football Hall of Fame?

   a. 1: Joe Namath

   b. 2: Joe Namath and Kurt Warner

   c. 3: Joe Namath, Kurt Warner, and Norm Van Brocklin

   d. 4: Joe Namath, Kurt Warner, Norm Van Brocklin, and Bob Waterfield

7. Roman Gabriel has played more games at quarterback for the Rams than any other player.

   a. True

   b. False

8. One journeyman Rams quarterback has been a part of eight NFL teams, more than any other quarterback who played for the Rams. Who was this well-travelled player?

   a. Case Keenum
   b. Josh McCown
   c. Chris Chandler
   d. Ryan Fitzpatrick

9. Which Ram was the youngest player in the team's history to start more than five games at quarterback, at just 22 years old?

   a. Jared Goff
   b. Norm Van Brocklin
   c. Billy Wade
   d. Sam Bradford

10. Which Los Angeles quarterback was moved to the Detroit Lions to make way for new quarterback Matthew Stafford when the Rams traded for Stafford in 2021?

    a. Sam Bradford
    b. Blake Bortles
    c. Jared Goff
    d. Case Keenum

11. How old was Rams quarterback Chris Chandler when he retired from his playing days in the NFL in 2004?

    a. 35 years old
    b. 37 years old
    c. 39 years old
    d. 41 years old

12. Rams quarterback Marc Bulger named previous quarterback Kurt Warner as the godfather when his daughter Cynthia Bulger was born in 2004.

   a. True
   b. False

13. The highest QBR (ESPN's Total Quarterback Rating) put up by a Los Angeles Ram for a full season was 63.6. Which quarterback scored this franchise high mark?

   a. Jared Goff
   b. Shaun Hill
   c. Sam Bradford
   d. Marc Bulger

14. Legendary Rams quarterback Kurt Warner is the only player who is a member of both the Pro Football Hall of Fame and the Arena Football Hall of Fame, because he started his career playing three seasons for which Arena Football League team?

   a. Atlantic City Blackjacks
   b. Columbus Destroyers
   c. Philadelphia Soul
   d. Iowa Barnstormers

15. Rams leader Tony Banks holds the franchise's record for most rushing yards in a season by a quarterback, which he set in 1996. How many yards did he rack up?

   a. 212
   b. 381

c. 540

d. 722

16. Rams quarterback Kurt Warner has won both a college national championship and a Super Bowl championship.

   a. True

   b. False

17. When Roman Gabriel was selected by the Rams in 1962, he became the first NFL quarterback to come from which background?

   a. Italian-American

   b. Brazilian-American

   c. Polish-American

   d. Filipino-American

18. Kurt Warner might have been a superstar with the Chicago Bears instead of the Rams, except that he was hampered before his Bears tryout in 1997 by what fluky occurrence?

   a. The death of his family's dog the morning of the tryout

   b. An ice storm that coated the field in Chicago

   c. A spider bite on his throwing elbow

   d. A sliver embedded in his thumb from a staircase railing at the facility

19. How many times did prolific Rams quarterback Roman Gabriel throw for 25 (or more) touchdowns in a single season?

a. 1

b. 3

c. 4

d. 6

20. Among quarterbacks who have started at least five games with Los Angeles, Dan Pastorini has the highest interception percentage, with 9.2% of his passes thrown being picked off.

a. True

b. False

QUIZ ANSWERS

1. D – Roman Gabriel

2. B – False

3. C – Bob Waterfield

4. D – Jim Everett

5. A – Kurt Warner

6. D – 4: Joe Namath, Kurt Warner, Norm Van Brocklin, and Bob Waterfield

7. A – True

8. D – Ryan Fitzpatrick

9. A – Jared Goff

10. C – Jared Goff

11. C – 39 years old

12. B – False

13. A – Jared Goff

14. D – Iowa Barnstormers

15. A – 212

16. B – False

17. D – Filipino-American

18. C – A spider bite on his throwing elbow

19. A – 1

20. A – True

DID YOU KNOW?

1. Frank Ryan owns the longest passing play in Rams history. He dropped back and found talented receiver Ollie Matson for a 96-yard touchdown toss that broke a tie during a 1961 matchup with the Pittsburgh Steelers and put the Rams ahead on the scoreboard for good.

2. Only one Rams quarterback has ever been able to complete 70% of his passes (minimum 100 thrown) in a season. The most accurate field general was Jaime Martin, who in 2005 managed to hit 70.1%.

3. Dieter Brock could have used some better blocking when he became the Rams' quarterback in 1985. He was sacked a whopping 51 times when he dropped back to pass; the highest total in Rams history.

4. Six quarterbacks who have started a game for the Rams have played their entire NFL careers with Los Angeles. Longest among them was Bob Waterfield, who spent eight seasons with the franchise from 1945 to 1952.

5. In an interesting coincidence, a large number of quarterbacks who have played for the Rams have also played for the Philadelphia Eagles. Some of the more notable players to have done so include Norm Van Brocklin, Roman Gabriel, Nick Foles, Sam Bradford, Dan Pastorini, and Ron Jaworski.

6. When NFL legend Bart Starr himself presented the Bart Starr Award for "outstanding character and leadership in the home, on the field, and in the community" to former Rams quarterback Kurt Warner in 2010, Starr said in his speech, "We have never given this award to anyone who was more deserving."

7. Rams quarterback Roman Gabriel was a major star in the 1960s. Taking advantage of Los Angeles's proximity to Hollywood, Gabriel appeared in such popular television shows as *Gilligan's Island*, *Perry Mason*, and *Wonder Woman*.

8. Los Angeles quarterback Jim Everett once had a memorable confrontation with sports talk show host Jim Rome. Rome poked fun at Everett's ability to take a sack and repeatedly called the quarterback "Chris," a reference to female tennis star Chris Evert. Everett lost his temper, flipped a table, and shoved Rome, knocking him to the ground.

9. Undrafted quarterback Kurt Warner had a storybook career, rising from obscurity to be thrust into a starting role after incumbent quarterback Trent Green suffered a preseason injury, then winning the NFL MVP, the Super Bowl, and Super Bowl MVP in his very first NFL season.

10. Quarterback Chris Chandler played for the Rams in both St. Louis and Los Angeles but was not with the team when they relocated. Instead, Chandler's stints with the team were a decade apart. He spent the 1994 season as an L.A. Ram, left the franchise to play in Houston, Atlanta,

and Chicago, and then returned to the Rams in St. Louis in 2004 to finish his playing career, but threw six interceptions in his second game.

CHAPTER 5:

THE PASS CATCHERS

QUIZ TIME!

1. Four wide receivers have recorded more than 45 career touchdown catches for the Rams. Which one of them has the most?

   a. Torry Holt
   b. Elroy Hirsch
   c. Henry Ellard
   d. Isaac Bruce

2. No one in Rams history is within 100 receptions of Isaac Bruce at the top of the Los Angeles record book.

   a. True
   b. False

3. Who is the Rams' single-season leader in receiving touchdowns scored, with 17?

   a. Torry Holt
   b. Isaac Bruce
   c. Elroy Hirsch
   d. Cooper Kupp

4. Who holds the all-time career franchise record for receiving yardage for the Rams?

   a. Isaac Bruce

   b. Jack Snow

   c. Torry Holt

   d. Henry Ellard

5. How did Rams receiver Flipper Anderson celebrate a game-winning touchdown in overtime against the New York Giants in a 1990 playoff matchup?

   a. He ran all the way back to midfield and laid the ball to rest on the Giants' logo.

   b. He hugged the goalpost, then shimmied up it and sat on the crossbar to take in the scene.

   c. He handed the ball to Giants coach Bill Parcells and gave Parcells a pat on the back and a wave goodbye.

   d. He ran into the end zone, then just kept going through the stadium tunnel and into the locker room.

6. Two Rams with at least 100 receptions have averaged 20 yards per catch over their careers. Which two have shown this amazing big play ability?

   a. Wide receiver Torry Holt and split end Del Shofner

   b. Wide receivers Isaac Bruce and Ron Jessie

   c. End Bob Boyd and wide receiver Flipper Anderson

   d. End Elroy Hirsch and wide receiver Harold Jackson

7. Rams wide receiver Cooper Kupp once attempted to set the world record for catching a football dropped from the

highest height but gave up after the fifth ball tossed from a hot air balloon high above glanced off his hand, fracturing one of Kupp's fingers.

a. True

b. False

8. Which Rams pass catcher has played more NFL games with the franchise than any other, with 197?

a. Tight end Bob Klein

b. Wide receiver Henry Ellard

c. Wide receiver Jack Snow

d. Wide receiver Isaac Bruce

9. Three pass catchers have over 500 career receptions for the Los Angeles Rams. Which of the following players is NOT among that club?

a. Tight end Lance Kendricks

b. Wide receiver Torry Holt

c. Wide receiver Henry Ellard

d. Wide receiver Isaac Bruce

10. Despite all his accomplishments, Henry Ellard has more career fumbles than any other Rams wide receiver. How many times did he cough up the ball?

a. 18

b. 25

c. 31

d. 40

11. According to Spotrac.com, which Rams wide receiver has played for the team on the contract with the highest total value, at $65 million?

    a. Isaac Bruce
    b. Cooper Kupp
    c. Torry Holt
    d. Robert Woods

12. Rams wide receiver Henry Ellard qualified for the 1992 Olympic trials in the triple jump.

    a. True
    b. False

13. How many Rams tight ends have caught over 200 passes for the club during their careers?

    a. 1: Lance Kendricks
    b. 2: Lance Kendricks and Billy Truax
    c. 4: Lance Kendricks, Billy Truax, Tyler Higbee, and Pete Holohan
    d. 5: Lance Kendricks, Billy Truax, Tyler Higbee, Pete Holohan, and Jared Cook

14. Which two teammates posted the highest combined receiving yardage total in a season for the Rams, reaching 3,106 yards together?

    a. Right end Elroy Hirsch and left end Tom Fears in 1951
    b. Wide receivers Henry Ellard and Flipper Anderson in 1989

c. Wide receivers Torry Holt and Isaac Bruce in 2000

d. Wide receivers Robert Woods and Cooper Kupp in 2019

15. Who was the Rams player that caught a game-winning 73-yard pass from quarterback Kurt Warner in Super Bowl XXXIV?

    a. Wide receiver Torry Holt

    b. Running back Marshall Faulk

    c. Wide receiver Ricky Proehl

    d. Wide receiver Isaac Bruce

16. Tavon Austin didn't just play wide receiver for the Rams, but also excelled as a kick returner. During the 2014 season, Austin had a streak of returning a kickoff or punt for a touchdown in five consecutive games.

    a. True

    b. False

17. Which of the following is NOT an NFL record held by Rams wide receiver Torry Holt?

    a. Most receiving yards per game for a career, with 77.4

    b. Most receiving yards in a decade, with 12,594 between 2000 and 2009

    c. Most yards per play gained in a single game, with 63 on September 24, 2000

    d. Most catches in a decade, with 868 between 2000 and 2009

18. Which Ram recorded the most catches in one season when he hauled in 119 passes for the squad?

a. Wide receiver Cooper Kupp

b. Left end Tom Fears

c. Wide receiver Isaac Bruce

d. Running back Steven Jackson

19. Which two teammates posted the highest touchdown reception total in a season for the Rams, converting 20 passes into scores?

   a. Right end Elroy Hirsch and left end Tom Fears in 1951

   b. Wide receiver Harold Jackson and running back Lawrence McCutcheon in 1973

   c. Wide receivers Isaac Bruce and Az-Zahir Hakim in 1999

   d. Both A and C are tied for the record.

20. In 2016, wide receivers Sammy Watkins and Robert Woods were starting for the Buffalo Bills. One season later, in 2017, Watkins and Woods were both teammates with the Los Angeles Rams after Watkins was traded there and Woods signed on as a free agent.

   a. True

   b. False

QUIZ ANSWERS

1. D – Isaac Bruce

2. B – False

3. C – Elroy Hirsch

4. A – Isaac Bruce

5. D – He ran into the end zone, then just kept going through the stadium tunnel and into the locker room.

6. C – End Bob Boyd and wide receiver Flipper Anderson

7. B – False

8. D – Wide receiver Isaac Bruce

9. A – Tight end Lance Kendricks

10. B – 25

11. D – Robert Woods

12. A – True

13. A – 1: Lance Kendricks

14. C – Wide receivers Torry Holt and Isaac Bruce in 2000

15. D – Wide receiver Isaac Bruce

16. B – False

17. A – Most receiving yards per game for a career, with 77.4

18. C – Wide receiver Isaac Bruce

19. D – Both A and C are tied for the record.

20. A – True

DID YOU KNOW?

1. Rams icon Isaac Bruce ranks fifth on the all-time list for most receiving yards in the history of the NFL, with 15,208. Bruce trails only Jerry Rice, Larry Fitzgerald, Terrell Owens, and Randy Moss.

2. The single-game record for most receptions in Los Angeles Rams history was set in 1950. End Tom Fears reeled in 18 passes against the Green Bay Packers to set the mark, which actually stood as an NFL record for half a century before being broken.

3. On Isaac Bruce's 30th birthday, November 10, 2002, the Rams wide receiver had a roller coaster of a game. Bruce fumbled the ball two times, but also scored three touchdowns including the game-winner as the Rams beat the San Diego Chargers, 28-24.

4. Some elite tight ends in NFL history have recorded more than 500 pass receptions. The Rams boast none of those tight ends. Lance Kendricks, who had 204 catches with the Rams and 244 overall, was less than halfway to that esteemed level.

5. No NFL player has ever totaled more receiving yards in a single game than Rams wideout Flipper Anderson did in a 1989 game against the New Orleans Saints. Anderson hauled in 15 passes for an astonishing 336 yards, a mark that still stands over 30 years later.

6. Four Los Angeles pass catchers share the team record for most receiving touchdowns in a single game, with four. This is just one off of the NFL's overall record of five. End Bob Shaw did it first in 1949, followed by halfback Elroy Hirsch in 1951, wide receiver Harold Jackson in 1973, and wide receiver Isaac Bruce in 1999.

7. In 1943, the Rams briefly disbanded because too many of their players had military duty during World War II. A dark time for the nation and the franchise turned into a career highlight for end Jim Benton though, as he was loaned to the Chicago Bears that year, won a world championship while there, and then rejoined the Rams the following season when they returned to play.

8. Los Angeles Rams receiver Jack Snow is the father of another successful athlete who played in California: Major League Baseball first baseman J.T. Snow, who starred with the San Francisco Giants and Los Angeles Angels.

9. Rams star wide receiver Elroy Hirsch had a wide variety of careers during his lifetime. In addition to being an NFL player, Hirsch was also a U.S. Marine, a film actor, a radio show host, general manager of the Rams, and an athletic director at the University of Wisconsin.

10. St. Louis-born rapper Nelly was passionate about both his hometown and its sports teams. Nelly featured Rams wide receiver Torry Holt in the video for his song "Air Force Ones," in which running back Marshall Faulk also appeared.

CHAPTER 6:

RUNNING WILD

QUIZ TIME!

1. Who holds the Rams' single-season franchise rushing yardage record after racking up 2,105 yards on the ground; the only time a Ram has cracked the 2,000-yard barrier?

   a. Jerome Bettis
   b. Eric Dickerson
   c. Marshall Faulk
   d. Todd Gurley

2. It is a Rams tradition for every running back to tap his helmet against the helmets of the starting offensive linemen following the warm-up before a game.

   a. True
   b. False

3. Which running back has accumulated the most carries for Los Angeles without ever scoring a rushing touchdown (167)?

a. Dante Magnani
b. Vitamin Smith
c. Daryl Richardson
d. Elvis Peacock

4. Which of the following accessories was superstar Rams running back Eric Dickerson most known for wearing on the field during games?

a. A gold Rolex watch under his wristband
b. Two diamond earrings in the shape of a "2" and a "9" (his jersey number) in his ears
c. A pair of prescription goggles over his eyes
d. His lucky neon-pink underwear under his uniform pants

5. How many running backs have carried the ball over 1,000 times for the Rams?

a. 2
b. 4
c. 6
d. 8

6. One Rams running back, with at least 16 games played, has averaged over 100 yards per game during his career with the team. Which player surpassed the century mark to average 111.5 yards per game?

a. Eric Dickerson
b. Steven Jackson
c. Lawrence Phillips
d. Marshall Faulk

7. The Rams have a set of ties at the top of their rushing touchdown leader board as Todd Gurley and Marshall Faulk have 58 rushing touchdowns apiece with the Rams, while Eric Dickerson and Steven Jackson have 56 each for Los Angeles.

    a. True
    b. False

8. In which season did fullback Dan Towler record an astonishing 6.8 yards per carry for Los Angeles?

    a. 1947
    b. 1951
    c. 1960
    d. 1972

9. Which Los Angeles running back (with at least 300 carries) has the highest career yards gained per attempt, with 5.5?

    a. Skeets Quinlan
    b. Dan Towler
    c. Fred Gehrke
    d. Tommy Wilson

10. Rams running back Cam Akers recorded his first NFL touchdown against which NFL team?

    a. New Orleans Saints
    b. Tampa Bay Buccaneers
    c. San Francisco 49ers
    d. New York Jets

11. How many of the Rams' top-10 seasons for rushing touchdowns were recorded by Hall of Fame running back Jerome Bettis?

   a. 0
   b. 2
   c. 3
   d. 5

12. The Rams have had at least one First Team All-Pro running back in every decade since the 1950s.

   a. True
   b. False

13. Which Los Angeles running back has the most career fumbles, with 51?

   a. Dick Bass
   b. Wendell Tyler
   c. Steven Jackson
   d. Eric Dickerson

14. Which Ram had the highest single-season rushing yards per game, reaching 131.6 (with a minimum of 100 carries)?

   a. Marshall Faulk
   b. Eric Dickerson
   c. Greg Hill
   d. Todd Gurley

15. After retiring from football as a St. Louis Ram in 2011, running back Cadillac Williams became a running backs coach in all of the following places, except for which one?

a. St. Louis Rams

b. IMG Academy White Team

c. Auburn Tigers

d. Birmingham Iron

16. Rams halfback Fred Gehrke is Major League Baseball MVP outfielder Christian Yelich's great-grandfather.

a. True

b. False

17. Popular website Football Nation stated that which Rams running back was "for a three-year period...the closest thing the NFL has ever produced to an unstoppable ball carrier"?

a. Eric Dickerson

b. Jerome Bettis

c. Dan Towler

d. Kenny Washington

18. Which of the following is NOT true about talented Rams running back Jerome Bettis?

a. Bettis did not play football until high school, because as a child, he preferred the sport of bowling.

b. Bettis admitted to selling drugs on the streets of Detroit in order to make some money during his adolescence.

c. Bettis was awarded the key to the city of Detroit, his hometown, by mayor Kwame Kilpatrick in 2006.

d. In retirement, Bettis donated a large amount to his alma mater, Notre Dame University, to fund a bus transportation system for students, which tied into his nickname "The Bus."

19. Only three NFL players have ever recorded 10,000 yards rushing and 5,000 yards receiving during their careers. Rams superstar Marshall Faulk is one; who are the other two running backs in that exclusive club?

    a. Roger Craig and Christian McCaffrey

    b. Charlie Garner and Le'Veon Bell

    c. Marcus Allen and Tiki Barber

    d. Herschel Walker and Alvin Kamara

20. When the Rams fired head coach Jeff Fisher and brought in Sean McVay to lead the team in 2017, running back Todd Gurley was thrilled. Gurley stated that Fisher's playbook had been like "running a middle school offense" in comparison to the innovative McVay.

    a. True

    b. False

QUIZ ANSWERS

1. B – Eric Dickerson

2. B – False

3. C – Daryl Richardson

4. C – A pair of prescription goggles over his eyes

5. C – 6

6. A – Eric Dickerson

7. A – True

8. B – 1951

9. D – Tommy Wilson

10. B – Tampa Bay Buccaneers

11. A – 0

12. B – False

13. D – Eric Dickerson

14. B – Eric Dickerson

15. A – St. Louis Rams

16. A – True

17. C – Dan Towler

18. D – In retirement, Bettis donated a large amount to his alma mater, Notre Dame University, to fund a bus

transportation system for students, which tied into his nickname "The Bus."

19. C – Marcus Allen and Tiki Barber

20. A – True

DID YOU KNOW?

1. Five running backs who have played for the Rams have been enshrined in the Pro Football Hall of Fame. The most recent was Jerome Bettis, who was elected in 2015.

2. Rams running back Marshall Faulk sits atop the NFL record book when it comes to most receiving yards in a season by a running back. Faulk piled up 1,048 yards in 1999, winning the NFL's Offensive Player of the Year Award for his production and versatility.

3. Eleven times in NFL history, a running back has scored 20 or more rushing touchdowns in a single season. Two Rams have gotten close to this mark, as Eric Dickerson reached 18 in 1983 and so did Marshall Faulk in 2000.

4. The NFL does not officially keep track of this statistic, but unofficially, surehanded Rams running back Steven Jackson is recognized as having the most consecutive touches without fumbling the ball. Jackson had 870 straight touches at the end of his career on which he did not give up possession of the football.

5. Los Angeles running back Marshall Faulk holds the NFL record for the most two-point conversions scored. Faulk notched seven of these high-pressure plays during his career.

6. Wendell Tyler led the L.A. Rams in rushing during Super Bowl XIV, and then did the same thing for the San

Francisco 49ers in Super Bowl XIX, making him the first player ever to accomplish that feat for two different teams.

7. Rams running back Paul "Tank" Younger was the first player from a predominantly black college (Grambling State University) to play in the NFL. Younger also later became the first African-American to work in an NFL front office, as he joined the Rams as a scout after his playing days ended.

8. Although Rams running back Eric Dickerson holds the official NFL record, there is some debate as to whether Dickerson's 1984 rushing total of 2,105 yards should be considered the benchmark. O.J. Simpson of the Buffalo Bills put up 2,003 rushing yards in 1983, and Simpson did it in a 14-game season, whereas the league had expanded to 16 games by the time Dickerson made his mark.

9. Most NCAA schools wanted Marshall Faulk to play cornerback. Little known San Diego State University offered him a scholarship as a running back, so Faulk went there to play for the Aztecs and finished in the top 10 in Heisman Trophy voting three times (finishing 2nd, 4th, and 9th) before his Hall of Fame career began.

10. Todd Gurley owns the Rams' record for most consecutive games with a touchdown. Gurley scored in 13 straight matchups to pass Elroy Hirsch as the leader.

CHAPTER 7:

IN THE TRENCHES

QUIZ TIME!

11. One Rams defender holds the team record by notching five sacks in a single game. Which defensive player was it?

    a. Defensive tackle Aaron Donald

    b. Defensive end Gary Jeter

    c. Linebacker James Laurinaitis

    d. Defensive end Kevin Greene

12. The 2016 Los Angeles Rams hold the NFL record for the heaviest combined weight of all starting offensive and defensive linemen.

    a. True

    b. False

13. Who is the Rams' all-time franchise leader in official sacks, having taken down opposing quarterbacks 87.5 times?

    a. Defensive tackle Aaron Donald

    b. Linebacker Kevin Greene

c. Defensive end Leonard Little

d. Defensive end Robert Quinn

14. Which offensive lineman did the Rams select highest in the NFL Entry Draft, using a 1st overall pick to add the stout blocker to their team?

    a. Tackle Orlando Pace

    b. Guard Tom Mack

    c. Tackle Greg Robinson

    d. Center Ed Beatty

15. Which offensive lineman has played more games (259) on the offensive side of the Rams' line of scrimmage than anyone else?

    a. Guard Joe Scibelli

    b. Tackle Charlie Cowan

    c. Center Doug Smith

    d. Tackle Jackie Slater

16. Which defensive lineman has played more games (208) on the defensive side of the Rams' line of scrimmage than anyone else?

    a. End Lamar Lundy

    b. Tackle Merlin Olsen

    c. End Jack Youngblood

    d. Tackle Michael Brockers

17. Rams defensive end Deacon Jones invented the now popularly used term "sack." It began as a play on words when the Rams were facing Dallas Cowboys quarterback

Craig Morton, who shared a surname with a famous brand of salt, and coach George Allen suggested the team "take that Morton salt and pour him into a sack," before Jones rephrased the idea to include all quarterbacks.

a. True
b. False

18. Which Rams defender showed the best nose for the ball, by leading the team in most career forced fumbles with 10 more than anyone else (31)?

a. Defensive end Robert Quinn
b. Defensive tackle Aaron Donald
c. Defensive end Leonard Little
d. Defensive tackle D'Marco Farr

19. Quarterback Roman Gabriel tops the record book for most fumbles recovered for the Rams, but he tended to be cleaning up his own mess. Which defenders have created the most turnovers for Los Angeles by scooping up an opponent's fumble 22 times each?

a. Safety Nolan Cromwell and defensive end Fred Dryer
b. Linebacker Jack Pardee and cornerback LeRoy Irvin
c. Defensive end Andy Robustelli and linebacker Les Richter
d. Safeties Johnnie Johnson and Eddie Meador

20. Offensive lineman Jackie Slater played his entire NFL career with the Los Angeles Rams after they took him in the 3rd round of the NFL Draft in 1976. How long did that career last?

a. 11 seasons

b. 14 seasons

c. 17 seasons

d. 20 seasons

21. Rams mainstay Orlando Pace played over 150 NFL games with the club. Where does he rank in games played all time for Los Angeles?

    a. 4th overall

    b. Tied for 9th overall

    c. Tied for 17th overall

    d. 23rd overall

22. Los Angeles defensive tackle Aaron Donald is the only player to win the NFL's Defensive Player of the Year Award in back-to-back seasons. He took home the trophy in 2018 and 2019.

    a. True

    b. False

23. Which current Rams defensive lineman has the longest tenure in Los Angeles?

    a. Tackle Aaron Donald

    b. Tackle Sebastian Joseph-Day

    c. End Jonah Williams

    d. Tackle A'Shawn Robinson

24. Which of the following professions did Rams Fearsome Foursome defensive tackle Rosey Grier NOT pursue in addition to his time as a football player?

a. Authoring a book about needlepoint
b. Singing on tour with Bob Hope and Ann-Margret
c. Speaking to congregations as a Protestant minister
d. Refereeing high school football games in his home state of Georgia

25. On which popular television show did Rams defensive tackle Merlin Olsen star for several seasons after his playing career ended?

a. *All in the Family*
b. *The Love Boat*
c. *Little House on the Prairie*
d. *M.A.S.H.*

26. Rams offensive lineman Rich Saul had a twin brother, Ron, who also played offensive line in the NFL for the Houston Oilers and Washington Redskins.

a. True
b. False

27. Which Rams lineman got to utter the noteworthy line "I'm a mountain man from West VA" in the team's 1986 promo video "Let's Ram It"?

a. Offensive tackle Bill Bain
b. Defensive end Doug Reed
c. Guard Dennis Harrah
d. Center Doug Smith

28. Which of the following is NOT true regarding the time that Hall of Fame left tackle Orlando Pace spent with the Rams from 1997 to 2008?

a. The offense accumulated more gross yards from scrimmage than any other NFL club during that time span (50,770 yards).

b. The offense produced three NFL MVP's: running back Marshall Faulk and quarterback Kurt Warner (twice).

c. Every single year, the passing game recorded at least 2,900 yards.

d. Pace was elected to the Pro Bowl every single season during that tenure, and achieved All-Pro status in half of those years.

29. Star Rams defensive end Merlin Olsen is tied for the NFL record after being chosen to represent his team in 14 Pro Bowls. Which of the following players does NOT share that record with Olsen?

a. Quarterback Peyton Manning of the Indianapolis Colts and Denver Broncos

b. Tight end Tony Gonzalez of the Kansas City Chiefs and Atlanta Falcons

c. Offensive lineman Bruce Matthews of the Houston Oilers

d. Linebacker Ray Lewis of the Baltimore Ravens

30. Rams defensive tackle Rosey Grier was a self-described "adrenaline junkie" who requested (and received) a clause in his contract allowing him to participate in activities such as bungee jumping, skydiving, and motorcycle racing. Grier was forced to stipulate that the

Rams would not be liable to pay him if he suffered an injury during any of those activities.

a. True
b. False

QUIZ ANSWERS

1. B – Defensive end Gary Jeter

2. B – False

3. C – Defensive end Leonard Little

4. A – Tackle Orlando Pace

5. D – Tackle Jackie Slater

6. B – Tackle Merlin Olsen

7. A – True

8. C – Defensive end Leonard Little

9. D – Safeties Johnnie Johnson and Eddie Meador

10. D – 20 seasons

11. C – Tied for 17th overall

12. B – False

13. A – Tackle Aaron Donald

14. D – Refereeing high school football games in his home state of Georgia

15. C – *Little House on the Prairie*

16. A – True

17. C – Guard Dennis Harrah

18. D – Pace was elected to the Pro Bowl every single season during that tenure, and achieved All-Pro status in half of those years

19. D – Linebacker Ray Lewis of the Baltimore Ravens

20. B – False

DID YOU KNOW?

1. In 1971 and 1972, the Rams fielded a lineup that was unique. Brothers Merlin and Phil Olsen both started right beside each other as defensive tackles for Los Angeles, marking the first time ever (and still the only time in league history) that this had happened.

2. When Rams great Eric Dickerson was elected to the Pro Football Hall of Fame in 1999, the running back gave full credit to his offensive line. He even went so far as to choose tackle Jackie Slater to be his presenter for the event.

3. Former Rams defensive tackle Rosy Grier became a bodyguard after retiring from the NFL and was the agent on duty who took down assassin Sirhan Sirhan after Robert F. Kennedy was fatally shot at the Ambassador Hotel during his 1968 campaign for the presidency.

4. Los Angeles defensive end Deacon Jones was a musical person who sang in a band that would later become famous as War. He also sang with Ray Charles, and had a song written about him: "Deacon Blues" by Steely Dan.

5. In 2009, mercurial St. Louis Rams guard Richie Incognito was voted by his peers as the dirtiest player in the NFL in a Sporting News poll. Complaints against him included illegal tackles, punching, and scratching opponents' eyes.

6. Rams defensive tackle Merlin Olsen and quarterback Roman Gabriel starred together on and off the field. Both

landed parts in a movie called *The Undefeated,* starring John Wayne, in 1969.

7. Defensive end Jack Youngblood was dubbed "The John Wayne of football" for his toughness and grit after continuing to play for the Rams through the 1979 NFL playoffs despite a fractured fibula in his left leg.

8. During the 2000 NFL season, the Rams' offensive line did an incredible job blocking. Not only did the team set a new NFL record for most passing yards in a season, but three members (left tackle Orlando Pace, right tackle Ryan Tucker, and center Andy McCollum) played the entire season without being called for a holding penalty even a single time.

9. Rams offensive lineman Tom Mack was the son of a professional athlete, but in baseball rather than football. Mack's father, Ray, played second base for the Cleveland Indians during the 1930s and '40s.

10. In 2018, Rams defensive tackle Aaron Donald signed a contract worth $135 million, the richest in NFL history for a player on the defensive side of the ball. The contract was eclipsed the very next day, however, when linebacker Khalil Mack signed with the Chicago Bears for $141 million.

CHAPTER 8:

THE BACK SEVEN

QUIZ TIME!

1. Which Rams safety is the franchise's all-time leader in interceptions, with 46?

   a. Eddie Meador

   b. Nolan Cromwell

   c. Todd Lyght

   d. Trumaine Johnson

2. During the 2010s poker craze, members of Los Angeles's secondary and linebacking corps held a weekly game where, rather than playing for money, the losers had to tweet embarrassing things about themselves or flattering things about the winners.

   a. True

   b. False

3. Three Rams players share the team's lead for most interceptions returned for a touchdown, with five apiece. Who are they?

a. Safety Nolan Cromwell and cornerbacks Rod Perry and Todd Lyght

b. Cornerbacks Jerry Gray, Trumaine Johnson, and Dré Bly

c. Safety Eddie Meador and cornerbacks LeRoy Irvin and Janoris Jenkins

d. Safety Johnnie Johnson and linebackers Jack Pardee and Jim Youngblood

4. Although sacks are usually not a high priority for defensive backs in most coaching systems, one Rams defensive back excelled at this skill, putting up 15 sacks in his career. Who?

a. Strong safety Adam Archuleta

b. Cornerback Todd Lyght

c. Free safety Keith Lyle

d. Cornerback Lamarcus Joyner

5. The initials in popular Rams free safety T.J. McDonald's name actually stand for what?

a. Terrance Jerome

b. Thomas Johnathan

c. Timothy Jr.

d. TerDarius Jamal

6. The Rams' record for most tackles made in a single season is 193. Which player set that high mark for the franchise?

a. Linebacker Alec Ogletree

b. Defensive tackle Aaron Donald

c. Linebacker James Laurinaitis

d. Linebacker London Fletcher

7. Los Angeles defensive back Nolan Cromwell married one of the Rams' cheerleaders. His wife, Mary Lynne Gehr, was also Miss Hollywood USA in 1980-81.

   a. True

   b. False

8. Which of the following is NOT true about quirky Rams linebacker Mel Owens?

   a. He established a law firm for which he was a partner, called Namanny, Byrne & Owens.

   b. He once participated in the notoriously dangerous running of the bulls in Pamplona, Spain.

   c. He applied to NASA in order to become an astronaut, but was turned down due to his age.

   d. He ran in and completed the Los Angeles Marathon in 1987.

9. Rams linebacker Kevin Greene was a firm supporter of the military; so much so that he enlisted and worked his way up to which rank?

   a. Corporal

   b. Captain

   c. Lieutenant

   d. General

10. All of the following facts about Rams linebacker Marlin McKeever are true, except for which of the following?

a. McKeever once had a role in a Three Stooges movie called *The Three Stooges Meet Hercules.*

b. McKeever often slept with headphones in on the night before a game, so that the game plan could better sink in while he was sleeping.

c. McKeever benefitted in his career from playing for five different coaches who were members of the Pro Football Hall of Fame.

d. McKeever once had a finger severed in a car accident caused by Rams quarterback Roman Gabriel.

11. Rams mainstay Jack Pardee played over 160 NFL games as a linebacker with the club. Where does he rank in games played all time for Los Angeles?

a. 3rd overall

b. Tied for 8th overall

c. 11th overall

d. Tied for 20th overall

12. Years after his playing and coaching careers were both over, Los Angeles linebacker Carl Ekern became a professor of sociology at Duke University.

a. True

b. False

13. Which of the following positions has popular Rams defensive back Nolan Cromwell NOT held after retiring from his playing career?

a. Special teams coordinator for the Green Bay Packers

b. Defensive assistant for the Los Angeles Rams

c. Wide receivers coach for the St. Louis Rams

d. Defensive backs coach for the Seattle Seahawks

14. Rams cornerback Clancy Williams worked with which Los Angeles institution after his playing career concluded?

a. The *Los Angeles Times* newspaper

b. The Los Angeles Police Department

c. The First Congregational Church of Los Angeles

d. The Los Angeles Unified School District

15. Which of the following facts about Rams defensive back Eddie Meador is NOT true?

a. He was elected to the Hall of Very Good in 2012 by the Professional Football Researchers Association.

b. He was the president of the NFL Players Association during his career.

c. For six consecutive seasons, he was selected as the L.A. Rams' Best Teammate by his fellow players.

d. In 1969, he was given the NFL Father of the Year Award.

16. In 1965, cornerback Irv Smith established the "Shutdown Time" tradition, wherein he donated his gold pocket watch upon retirement to the next cornerback to take up the mantle for Los Angeles. To this day, the watch hangs in a cornerback's locker, and he must pass it on if he retires, is traded, cut, or signs elsewhere.

a. True

b. False

17. Which Los Angeles Rams defensive back was also drafted by Major League Baseball's New York Yankees before choosing a football career instead?

    a. Safety Dave Elmendorf
    b. Cornerback Todd Lyght
    c. Cornerback Jerry Gray
    d. Safety Keith Lyle

18. Colorful Rams linebacker Kevin Greene once appeared in the main event of a wrestling pay per view, WCW's *Slamboree*, as a tag team partner of which two famous wrestling superstars?

    a. Macho Man Randy Savage and Ravishing Rick Rude
    b. The Nature Boy Ric Flair and Rowdy Roddy Piper
    c. Mr. Perfect Curt Hennig and Hulk Hogan
    d. Sting and Lex Luger

19. When Rams linebacker Mel Owens started up a telephone service in the 1980s to help citizens nationwide make restaurant reservations, what was the phone number he used for the service?

    a. 1-800-DINE-OUT
    b. 1-800-FOOD-GUY
    c. 1-800-BOOK-YUM
    d. 1-800-LETS-EAT

20. Rams linebacker Jack Pardee was one of the "Junction Boys"; a group of Texas A&M football players made famous in books and film because of a grueling training camp conducted by the legendary coach Bear Bryant.

a. True

b. False

QUIZ ANSWERS

1. A – Eddie Meador

2. B – False

3. C – Safety Eddie Meador and cornerbacks LeRoy Irvin and Janoris Jenkins

4. A – Strong safety Adam Archuleta

5. C – Timothy Jr.

6. D – Linebacker London Fletcher

7. A – True

8. C – He applied to NASA in order to become an astronaut, but was turned down due to his age.

9. B – Captain

10. B – McKeever often slept with headphones in on the night before a game, so that the game plan could better sink in while he was sleeping.

11. C – 11th overall

12. B – False

13. D – Defensive backs coach for the Seattle Seahawks

14. A – The *Los Angeles Times* newspaper

15. C – For six consecutive seasons, he was selected as the L.A. Rams' Best Teammate by his fellow players.

16. B – False

17. A – Safety Dave Elmendorf

18. B – The Nature Boy Ric Flair and Rowdy Roddy Piper

19. D – 1-800-LETS-EAT

20. A – True

DID YOU KNOW?

1. Passes defended is a stat that the NFL began using at the turn of the century. Cornerback Trumaine Johnson has led the statistic for the Rams, having knocked down 67. Cornerback Ron Bartell is second on the team, with 60.

2. Rams cornerback Dexter McCleon was not easily impressed by opponents. Once, during the Super Bowl in 2002, McCleon was caught on film saying to teammates "Tom Brady...overrated." Brady, then the quarterback of the opposing New England Patriots, is frequently considered the best football player of all time.

3. Linebacker James Laurinaitis is the all-time leading tackler for the Rams franchise. Laurinaitis played in Los Angeles for seven seasons and racked up 1,015 tackles during that time.

4. Cornerback Cortland Finnegan made quite the first impression with the Rams. After signing with St. Louis as a free agent in 2012, Finnegan not only intercepted a pass in his first game with the team, but also ran it back for a touchdown.

5. Linebacker Kevin Greene holds the Los Angeles record for most safeties created, with three of them during his Rams career.

6. Former Rams linebacker Roman Phifer had some regrets about his playing days due to the lingering effects that he

felt physically in retirement. Phifer produced a well-respected documentary film called *Blood Equity* that featured other former players discussing the impacts of the physical trauma they had been through.

7. Two defensive backs who have played for the Rams have been enshrined in the Football Hall of Fame. The most recent was Aeneas Williams, who was elected in 2014.

8. When rookie defensive back Johnnie Johnson signed a $1 million contract with the Rams in 1980, it caused a major ripple effect. Many of the team's veterans did not appreciate the rookie earning so much, and defensive end Jack Youngblood, linebacker Jim Youngblood, defensive tackle Larry Brooks, and offensive lineman Dennis Harrah all engaged in contract holdouts as a result.

9. Former Rams linebacker Jack Pardee holds the distinction of being the only person to coach a football team in the NFL, CFL, NCAA, USFL, and WFL. Pardee accomplished this through his jobs with the Houston Oilers, Chicago Bears, Washington Redskins, Birmingham Barracudas, Houston Cougars, Houston Gamblers, and Florida Blazers.

10. Rams linebacker Les Richter excelled at nearly everything he did. Not only was Richter elected to the College Football Hall of Fame and Pro Football Hall of Fame; he was also honored by the Motorsports Hall of Fame of America for his work as senior vice president of operations with NASCAR.

CHAPTER 9:

WHERE'D THEY COME FROM?

QUIZ TIME!

1. Where was legendary Rams defensive end Deacon Jones born?

   a. Cedar Rapids, Iowa

   b. Poughkeepsie, New York

   c. Eatonville, Florida

   d. Toronto, Ontario

2. Los Angeles Rams defensive back Todd Lyght, who played for a decade with the team, is the only NFL player ever who was born in Marshall Islands.

   a. True

   b. False

3. In 1952, the Rams chose three players from one college in back-to-back-to-back rounds. Where did guard Duane Putnam, tackle Burt Delavan, and halfback Tom McCormick all go to school?

   a. University of Notre Dame

   b. Washington State University

c. University of Oklahoma

d. University of the Pacific

4. The Rams twice made trades involving cornerback Aqib Talib. Which team did they acquire him from, and which team did they send him to?

   a. Acquired from the Denver Broncos, traded to the Miami Dolphins

   b. Acquired from the Tampa Bay Buccaneers, traded to the Denver Broncos

   c. Acquired from the New England Patriots, traded to the Miami Dolphins

   d. Acquired from the Tampa Bay Buccaneers, traded to the New England Patriots

5. From which team did the Rams acquire useful defensive end Dante Fowler Jr. in a 2018 swap?

   a. Seattle Seahawks

   b. Kansas City Chiefs

   c. Jacksonville Jaguars

   d. New York Jets

6. Which of the following is NOT an actual college program that Los Angeles drafted a player from during the 1970 NFL Draft?

   a. Prairie View A&M Panthers

   b. Missouri A&M Marauders

   c. Florida A&M Rattlers

   d. West Texas A&M Buffaloes

7. The Rams have drafted more players from the Michigan State Spartans than from the Michigan Wolverines over the course of their history.

   a. True
   b. False

8. Which high-profile player acquired in a trade by the Rams was released by the club, and then returned to his original team where he went on to become the Super Bowl MVP?

   a. Wide receiver Hines Ward of the Pittsburgh Steelers
   b. Safety Dexter Jackson of the Tampa Bay Buccaneers
   c. Quarterback Nick Foles of the Philadelphia Eagles
   d. Quarterback Mark Rypien of the Washington Redskins

9. One of the Rams' best recent trades saw them acquire cornerback Marcus Peters, in exchange for a 2nd and 4th round draft pick. Which team made that deal with Los Angeles?

   a. Baltimore Ravens
   b. Jacksonville Jaguars
   c. New Orleans Saints
   d. Kansas City Chiefs

10. In which commonly named city was Rams franchise quarterback Kurt Warner born in 1971?

   a. Burlington, California
   b. Burlington, Iowa
   c. Burlington, Kansas
   d. Burlington, Michigan

11. Two players were teammates within the same position group in college with the West Virginia Mountaineers before taking the field together in Los Angeles as well. Which two players were they?

    a. Wide receivers Tavon Austin and Steadman Bailey
    b. Tight ends Tyler Higbee and Temarrick Hemingway
    c. Defensive backs Janoris Jenkins and Trumaine Johnson
    d. Linebackers Robert Thomas and Courtland Bullard

12. Los Angeles has never in its history completed a trade with the Jacksonville Jaguars.

    a. True
    b. False

13. Rams linebacker Shane Conlan won two national championships and made the College Football Hall of Fame as a member of which program before his time in Los Angeles?

    a. Florida State Seminoles
    b. Nebraska Cornhuskers
    c. Penn State Nittany Lions
    d. USC Trojans

14. In 1959, the Rams drafted future Pro Bowl safety Ed Meador, who played for Arkansas Tech University, in the 7th round. What was his college team's unusual nickname?

    a. The Pterodactyls
    b. The Squealin' Hogs

c. The Astronauts

d. The Wonder Boys

15. The football stadium at which university is named Merlin Olsen Stadium, after the famous Rams defensive tackle and school alumnus?

a. Utah State University

b. University of Oklahoma

c. University of California - Santa Barbara

d. Fordham University

16. In their entire history, the Rams have never traded away a player who was born in the state of California.

a. True

b. False

17. Which college program did Mexican split end Tom Fears attend before his entrance into the NFL in 1945?

a. Florida Gators

b. Texas Longhorns

c. UCLA Bruins

d. UNLV Runnin' Rebels

18. From which other team did the Rams poach star left tackle Andrew Whitworth as a free agent in 2017?

a. New York Giants

b. Detroit Lions

c. Denver Broncos

d. Cincinnati Bengals

19. The talented and flamboyant Dante Hall was a member of which college squad before his time on the field with the Rams?

    a. USC Trojans
    b. Florida State Seminoles
    c. Alabama Crimson Tide
    d. Texas A&M Aggies

20. Los Angeles has completed more trades with the Dallas Cowboys than with any other NFL franchise.

    a. True
    b. False

QUIZ ANSWERS

1. C – Eatonville, Florida

2. A – True

3. D – University of the Pacific

4. A – Acquired from the Denver Broncos, traded to the Miami Dolphins

5. C – Jacksonville Jaguars

6. B – Missouri A&M Marauders

7. A – True

8. C – Quarterback Nick Foles of the Philadelphia Eagles

9. D – Kansas City Chiefs

10. B – Burlington, Iowa

11. A – Wide receivers Tavon Austin and Steadman Bailey

12. B – False

13. C – Penn State Nittany Lions

14. D – The Wonder Boys

15. A – Utah State University

16. B – False

17. C – UCLA Bruins

18. D – Cincinnati Bengals

19. D – Texas A&M Aggies

20. B – False

DID YOU KNOW?

1. When the Rams decided to switch to a more pass-based offense in 1996, they needed to trade power running back Jerome Bettis away from St. Louis because he did not want to switch to fullback. The franchise offered him the choice of a few teams and sent him to the Pittsburgh Steelers at his request, getting just a 2nd and 4th round pick in return for the future Hall-of-Famer.

2. Rams tight end Terry Nelson was lucky to be noticed by NFL scouts. Nelson played at the University of Arkansas at Pine Bluff, a school that did not traditionally receive much attention from NFL teams in those days.

3. Rams kicker Carlos Huerta was well-travelled during his football career. Huerta played for two teams in the National Football League, two teams in the Arena Football League, and three teams in the Canadian Football League.

4. Superstar wide receiver Isaac Bruce made it to the Pro Football Hall of Fame after his excellent Rams career. In doing so, Bruce became the only player from the University of Memphis ever to be inducted.

5. One of the best trades made by the Rams occurred in 1999 when they sent two future draft choices to the Indianapolis Colts for disgruntled running back Marshall

Faulk. Faulk was unhappy with his contract in Indianapolis, but signed a new one with the Rams and quickly helped lead them to a Super Bowl as part of one of the best offenses in league history.

6. In a decision that was somewhat controversial at the time, Los Angeles signed free agent defensive tackle Ndamukong Suh in 2018. Suh had a bit of a checkered past and was considered by many to be a dirty player, but his presence was a major help to Rams star Aaron Donald and definitely paid off on the field.

7. One of the larger and more impactful trades ever made by the Rams was completed on Halloween in 1987. It was a three-team deal that also involved the Indianapolis Colts and Buffalo Bills. Buffalo sent running back Greg Bell, a 1988 1st round draft choice, and 1st and 2nd round draft choices in 1989 to Los Angeles and received linebacker Cornelius Bennett in the blockbuster. Los Angeles also received running back Owen Gil, 1st and 2nd round draft picks in 1988, and a 2nd round draft choice in 1989 from Indianapolis, while the Colts got superstar running back Eric Dickerson from the Rams.

8. Fan-favorite quarterback Ron Jaworski is the only player the Rams have ever selected who played college football for the Youngstown State Penguins.

9. Tom Fears broke a barrier when the Rams selected him in the 1945 NFL Draft, as he became the first player born in Mexico to be chosen by an NFL franchise. Although he

was chosen as a defensive back, Los Angeles converted him to a split end where he enjoyed tremendous success, later becoming the first Mexico-born player elected to the Pro Football Hall of Fame.

10. Los Angeles hit the jackpot when they chose offensive tackle Jackie Slater in the 3rd round, 86th overall in the 1976 NFL Draft. For such a low pick, Slater paid huge dividends and eventually ended up in the Pro Football Hall of Fame.

CHAPTER 10:

IN THE DRAFT ROOM

QUIZ TIME!

1. Johnny Drake, the Rams' first-ever draft choice, attended Purdue University, where he played for the football team that went by which nickname?

   a. Turbochargers
   b. Pirates
   c. Boilermakers
   d. Coastal Coyotes

2. For the last five consecutive years, the Rams have traded out of the 1st round of the NFL Draft, acquiring more proven talent in an effort to win quickly.

   a. True
   b. False

3. From which of the following college football programs in Texas have the Rams drafted the most players?

   a. Texas Longhorns
   b. Texas Tech Red Riders

c. Texas A&M Aggies

d. Texas El Paso Miners

4. During the 2nd round of the 2020 NFL Draft, Los Angeles congratulated which of the following players on becoming a Ram remotely, via webcam, because of the COVID-19 pandemic that prevented the usual handshakes on stage?

a. Defensive end K'Lavon Chaisson of the LSU Tigers

b. Safety Taylor Rapp of the Washington Huskies

c. Running back Cam Akers of the Florida State Seminoles

d. Linebacker Terrell Lewis of the Alabama Crimson Tide

5. The Rams selected two teammates from the Washington Huskies in the 2019 NFL Draft. Which teammates did they choose with the 61st and 134th picks?

a. Safety Nick Scott and running back John Kelly

b. Tight end Gerald Everett and wide receiver Cooper Kupp

c. Wide receiver Pharoah Cooper and linebacker Bryce Hager

d. Safety Taylor Rapp and defensive tackle Greg Gaines

6. How many times in history has Los Angeles used a top 10 overall draft pick?

a. 25

b. 37

c. 44

d. 52

7. When the Rams selected star defensive end Leonard Little with the 65th pick in the 1998 NFL Draft, they did so at the last minute. St. Louis made a trade with the Pittsburgh Steelers to obtain the pick *while* Steelers coach Bill Cowher was on the phone with Little welcoming him to Pittsburgh.

   a. True
   b. False

8. Defensive end Robert Quinn was drafted by the Rams out of which school that is better known as a basketball powerhouse than a football school?

   a. Duke University
   b. University of North Carolina
   c. University of Kentucky
   d. Gonzaga University

9. Superstar running back Eric Dickerson was drafted by Los Angeles 2nd overall in the 1983 NFL Draft. Which excellent player, who also made the Hall of Fame, was selected ahead of him?

   a. Offensive tackle Jimbo Covert
   b. Quarterback Dan Marino
   c. Defensive back Darrell Green
   d. Quarterback John Elway

10. Only one Ivy League player from Harvard University has played for the Rams after being drafted by them. Which intelligent player made it with Los Angeles?

a. Quarterback Ryan Fitzpatrick

b. Linebacker Marlin McKeever

c. Offensive tackle Jason Smith

d. Tight end Bob Klein

11. How high did Los Angeles select Heisman Trophy winner Eric Crouch in the 2002 NFL Draft?

    a. 1st round, 6th overall

    b. 2nd round, 39th overall

    c. 3rd round, 95th overall

    d. 7th round, 224th overall

12. Due in part to their longstanding rivalry with the San Francisco 49ers, Los Angeles has never drafted a player from the Stanford Cardinal.

    a. True

    b. False

13. How many draft choices did the Rams give up to the Tennessee Titans in order to move up and select quarterback Jared Goff in the 2016 NFL Draft?

    a. 3

    b. 4

    c. 6

    d. 8

14. Wide receiver Flipper Anderson played four years of college ball for which local program before being drafted by the Rams?

    a. University of California Golden Bears

    b. San Jose State Spartans

c. USC Trojans

d. UCLA Bruins

15. The Rams drafted two players from the Auburn Tigers who would go on to play more than 200 NFL games each. Who were these players?

   a. Linebacker Kevin Greene and offensive tackle Wayne Gandy

   b. Kicker Jim Bakken and running back Jerrel Wilson

   c. Linebacker Roman Phifer and wide receiver Harold Jackson

   d. Defensive tackle Ryan Pickett and guard Joe Scibelli

16. Rams defensive tackle Aaron Donald was such a talented athlete coming out of college that he was drafted in not one but three sports (basketball, baseball, and football).

   a. True

   b. False

17. Which team did the Rams trade up with so they could select future Hall of Fame left tackle Orlando Pace 1st overall at the NFL Draft in 1997?

   a. Cincinnati Bengals

   b. New Orleans Saints

   c. New York Jets

   d. Detroit Lions

18. In the 1992 NFL Draft, Los Angeles selected not one but two quarterbacks. Who did they take to attempt to lock down the position?

a. Jeff Carlson and Hugh Millen

b. Ryan Fitzpatrick and Joe Germaine

c. Marc Bulger and Geoff Puddester

d. Ricky Jones and T.J. Rubley

19. Who did the Los Angeles Rams select with their three 1st round draft picks in 2001?

a. Safety Adam Archuleta and defensive tackles Damione Lewis and Ryan Pickett

b. Running back Trung Canidate, wide receiver Torry Holt, and cornerback Dré Bly

c. Defensive end Grant Wistrom, wide receiver Az-Zahir Hakim, and linebacker Tommy Polley

d. Linebacker Robert Thomas, defensive tackle Jimmy Kennedy, and running back Steven Jackson

20. Between 2000 and 2010, Los Angeles enjoyed a stretch in which they selected at least one player per year who lasted 100 games in the NFL.

a. True

b. False

QUIZ ANSWERS

1. C – Boilermakers

2. A – True

3. A – Texas Longhorns

4. C – Running back Cam Akers of the Florida State Seminoles

5. D – Safety Taylor Rapp and defensive tackle Greg Gaines

6. D – 52

7. A – True

8. B – University of North Carolina

9. D – Quarterback John Elway

10. A – Quarterback Ryan Fitzpatrick

11. C – 3rd round, 95th overall

12. B – False

13. C – 6

14. D – UCLA Bruins

15. A – Linebacker Kevin Greene and offensive tackle Wayne Gandy

16. B – False

17. C – New York Jets

18. D – Ricky Jones and T.J. Rubley

19. A – Safety Adam Archuleta and defensive tackles Damione Lewis and Ryan Pickett

20. B – False

DID YOU KNOW?

1. Center Donn Moomaw, who was chosen 9th overall in 1953, is the highest drafted player the Rams have ever selected from the UCLA Bruins.

2. The most players Los Angeles has drafted from any school is 44. This mark is held by the UCLA Bruins, who are slightly ahead of the University of Southern California Trojans and University of Washington Huskies for the lead.

3. Los Angeles has held the 50th overall pick a dozen times; more than any other spot in the draft. They have selected at this spot at least once in every decade except the 1950s and 1990s.

4. Los Angeles has made two Baylor Bears players top two picks in the NFL Draft. The team selected halfback Jack Wilson 2nd overall in 1942 and tackle Jason Smith 2nd overall in 2009.

5. The Rams have drafted 11 players from the University of Missouri, including four while the franchise was located in St. Louis. One of these players was defensive end Michael Sam, who became the first openly gay player drafted by an NFL team in 2014.

6. Los Angeles has drafted precisely 22 players who have played a single game in the NFL. While the majority come

from the team's early years, defensive end Ejuan Price was the most recent after his selection in 2017.

7. Of the draft spots in the top 10 in the NFL Draft, Los Angeles has selected at 2nd overall more than any other, choosing nine players in that position. Best among them were Hall of Fame running back Eric Dickerson and Hall of Fame guard Tom Mack.

8. The smallest-ever draft classes selected by the Rams in the NFL Draft were six members each. These came in 1997 (when they took franchise tackle Orlando Pace) and 2016 (when they chose franchise quarterback Jared Goff).

9. The largest Rams draft class ever was selected in 1956, when the team drafted 36 players over the course of the draft. Four of those players lasted over 100 games in the NFL, including 1st round pick Joe Marconi and 28th round pick John Morrow.

10. The latest pick the Rams have made in the NFL Draft was defensive back Gary Shaw from BYU, whom the team chose 485th overall in 1976. Shaw never made it to the NFL. Wide receiver Joe Sweet, the team's 435th overall pick from Tennessee State in 1971, was the latest pick they've made who actually played for the team.

CHAPTER 11:

COACHES, GMS, & OWNERS

QUIZ TIME!

1. Who served as the Rams' first general manager?

   a. Billy Evans

   b. Jack Teele

   c. Dutch Clark

   d. Don Klosterman

2. Los Angeles general manager Charley Armey once proposed a deal to the New England Patriots that would have sent Rams icon Kurt Warner to Massachusetts in exchange for a young and then little-known Tom Brady.

   a. True

   b. False

3. The Rams' first head coach, Damon Wetzel, lasted for how long in that position with the franchise?

   a. 3 games

   b. 9 games

   c. 38 games

   d. 62 games

4. The Rams' most recent coach, Sean McVay, rose through the coaching ranks by taking positions at all of the following franchises except for which one?

   a. Ohio State Buckeyes
   b. Washington Football Team
   c. Florida Tuskers
   d. Tampa Bay Buccaneers

5. Rams owner Stan Kroenke married Ann Walton, the heiress to which lucrative corporation?

   a. McDonald's
   b. Nike
   c. Budweiser
   d. Walmart

6. Who was the offensive coordinator for the Rams during their "Greatest Show on Turf" era, during which the team set records, claimed NFL MVP awards, and won a Super Bowl?

   a. Sean McVay
   b. Mike Martz
   c. Dick Vermeil
   d. Jeff Fisher

7. Los Angeles is the only NFL franchise to have a player rise from competing on the field for the team to ownership of the team.

   a. True
   b. False

8. Which coach led the Rams to their first-ever NFL championship?

   a. Joe Stydahar
   b. Dick Vermeil
   c. Adam Walsh
   d. Sean McVay

9. Which of the following Los Angeles general managers once took the field as a player on the team before getting the chance to guide it from the front office?

   a. Elroy Hirsch
   b. Dick Vermeil
   c. Dan Reeves
   d. Les Snead

10. Who is the Los Angeles leader in all-time coaching wins with the franchise, with 75 in the regular season and 79 including playoff victories?

    a. Chuck Knox
    b. Mike Martz
    c. John Robinson
    d. Ray Malavasi

11. How old was current Rams head coach Sean McVay when Los Angeles hired him in 2017, and he became the youngest head coach of the NFL's modern era?

    a. 26 years old
    b. 30 years old
    c. 34 years old
    d. 41 years old

12. Coach Mike Martz's 2001 season is the franchise benchmark in terms of regular season wins, as he led the team to 14 of them that year against only two defeats.

   a. True
   b. False

13. To date, how many of the Rams' head coaches have spent their entire NFL head coaching career with Los Angeles?

   a. 2
   b. 5
   c. 8
   d. 12

14. Which Rams general manager has led the franchise to eight playoff appearances; the most of any of the team's GMs?

   a. Dan Reeves
   b. Charley Armey
   c. Don Klosterman
   d. John Shaw

15. The legendary Chuck Knox had two stints coaching the Rams. How many years elapsed between those two terms?

   a. 3
   b. 7
   c. 10
   d. 15

16. At one point in their history, the Rams employed four coaches over a decade who had all started for Los Angeles at some point during their playing careers.

a. True

b. False

17. How did Georgia Frontiere become the majority owner of the Rams, and the only active female owner in the NFL, in 1979?

    a. She purchased the team when the previous owners wished to sell.

    b. She inherited the team from her husband.

    c. She forced a takeover of the corporation that had previously owned the team.

    d. She was hired as CEO of the company that owned the team.

18. How many head coaches have roamed the sidelines for the Rams in their history?

    a. 12

    b. 19

    c. 28

    d. 34

19. All of the following Rams coaches won an Associated Press award as the league's top coach, but which was the only one to do so behind the bench while the team was located in St. Louis?

    a. Chuck Knox

    b. Sean McVay

    c. George Allen

    d. Dick Vermeil

20. Rams owner Georgia Frontiere once proposed trading franchises with New York Yankees owner George Steinbrenner, as part of a business deal.

   a. True
   b. False

QUIZ ANSWERS

1. C – Dutch Clark

2. B – False

3. B – 9 games

4. A – Ohio State Buckeyes

5. D – Walmart

6. B – Mike Martz

7. B – False

8. C – Adam Walsh

9. A – Elroy Hirsch

10. C – John Robinson

11. B – 30 years old

12. A – True

13. D – 12

14. C – Don Klosterman

15. D – 15

16. B – False

17. B – She inherited the team from her husband.

18. C – 28

19. D – Dick Vermeil

20. B – False

DID YOU KNOW?

1. Five times in team history, the Rams fired a coach midway through a season. Most recently, this happened in 2016 when Jeff Fisher was released with three games to play. John Fassell took over the team and went 0-3 to finish the year.

2. Only two men have served as both coach and general manager of the Rams. Dutch Clark was the first in the franchise's early days. Most recently, Dick Vermeil was given that control and held the dual role from 1997 to 1999.

3. Current Rams owner Stan Kroenke is one of the wealthiest NFL owners, and has expanded his investments portfolio to several other sports franchises, including: Arsenal F.C. of the Premier League, Arsenal W.F.C. of the Women's Super League, the Colorado Avalanche of the National Hockey League, the Denver Nuggets of the National Basketball Association, the Colorado Mammoth of the National Lacrosse League, the Colorado Rapids of Major League Soccer, the Los Angeles Guerillas of the Call of Duty League, and the Los Angeles Gladiators of the Overwatch League.

4. The Rams' original general manager, Dutch Clark, lasted two seasons, 1939 and 1940. Clark would go on to become a Hall-of-Famer as a player and wanted to play for the

Rams while also coaching and managing the team. However, his playing rights were held by the Detroit Lions, and no agreement was reached to allow him to take the field for the Rams.

5. Rams head coach Jeff Fisher racked up 45 losses with the franchise. Those, in addition to his losses with the Houston Oilers/Tennessee Titans, give Fisher 165 regular season defeats in total, which is tied with Dan Reeves as the NFL's all-time record for most losses by a head coach.

6. Three "Bills" have served as general manager of the Rams, all at least 30 years apart, and none for a long tenure. Billy Evans had the role during World War II in 1941. When the 1970s began, Bill Barnes held the title for the 1971 season. And in 2009, Billy Devaney took over and outlasted the others by remaining at the helm for three seasons.

7. Mike Martz was an excellent head coach for the Rams, as affirmed by his .624 winning percentage and his quarterback Marc Bulger, who said, "He was by far the smartest football mind I've ever been around." Martz, unfortunately, contracted a bacterial infection of the heart in 2005 that led him to step down from his coaching duties.

8. The Rams are one of few NFL franchises to employ a head coach who was born outside the United States. Second-ever Rams coach Hugo Bezdek, who led the team in 1937 and part of 1938, was born in Prague in 1884. Bezdek is also unique in that he once managed the Pittsburgh

Pirates, a Major League Baseball team, before joining the Rams.

9. Before becoming the commissioner of the NFL for three decades, Pete Rozelle was once the general manager of the Los Angeles Rams for three seasons.

10. Only once in league history has a Los Angeles general manager been awarded the Sporting News NFL Executive of the Year Award. Dan Reeves received the honor in 1955, which was the first year it was ever given out.

CHAPTER 12:

ODDS & ENDS

QUIZ TIME!

1. Which Ram has won the most Associated Press MVP trophies while playing for Los Angeles?

    a. Quarterback Roman Gabriel

    b. Running back Marshall Faulk

    c. Defensive tackle Aaron Donald

    d. Quarterback Kurt Warner

2. The first Ram to win any major award given out by the NFL was franchise quarterback Norm Van Brocklin.

    a. True

    b. False

3. During which season did the Rams win their first Vince Lombardi Trophy as Super Bowl champions?

    a. 1963

    b. 1984

    c. 1999

    d. 2002

4. In 2019, the NFL announced its All-Time Team, recognizing the 100 greatest players from the first 100 years of NFL history. How many of these players suited up for the Rams?

   a. 2 on offense, 3 on defense, and 0 on special teams
   b. 3 on offense, 1 on defense, and 1 on special teams
   c. 5 on offense, 4 on defense, and 1 on special teams
   d. 4 on offense, 2 on defense, and 0 on special teams

5. Who is the only Los Angeles Ram to persevere through a negative event before returning to the Rams to win the NFL Comeback Player of the Year Award?

   a. Quarterback Kurt Warner in 2004
   b. Defensive end Deacon Jones in 1972
   c. Running back Dick Bass in 1966
   d. Wide receiver Cooper Kupp in 2019

6. What is J.B. Long's connection to the Los Angeles Rams?

   a. An architect who designed and built SoFi Stadium for the Rams
   b. A beloved groundskeeper who has worked for the Rams since 1992
   c. A player agent who represented Aaron Donald, Todd Gurley, and several others
   d. A play-by-play radio announcer for the Rams on their home station

7. The Los Angeles Rams have the most wins of any franchise in NFL history.

   a. True
   b. False

8. Which Rams kicker (with at least 50 kicks attempted) holds the team's highest field goal percentage, at 82% made?

   a. Greg Zuerlein
   b. Jeff Wilkins
   c. Mike Lansford
   d. Josh Brown

9. Only one Rams player has ever won the NFL's Defensive Player of the Year Award, but he has won it three times, which is tied for the league record. Which player took home that trophy so often?

   a. Defensive end Deacon Jones
   b. Linebacker Leonard Little
   c. Defensive tackle Aaron Donald
   d. Defensive tackle Merlin Olsen

10. Against which opposing team does the Rams franchise have the most playoff victories?

   a. Minnesota Vikings
   b. Philadelphia Eagles
   c. New England Patriots
   d. Dallas Cowboys

11. Kicker Greg Zuerlein holds the franchise record for the longest field goal made, which was set against the Minnesota Vikings in 2015. How long was this record-setting kick?

   a. 58 yards
   b. 59 yards

c. 61 yards

d. 63 yards

12. Los Angeles is the first NFL team to win the Super Bowl after losing the previous year.

a. True

b. False

13. In their four appearances, what is the most points the Rams have scored in any Super Bowl?

a. 17

b. 23

c. 30

d. 42

14. Of the Rams in the Football Hall of Fame, quarterback Bob Waterfield is first among them to play with the Rams. What year did he begin playing with the team?

a. 1945

b. 1951

c. 1963

d. 1966

15. Three Rams have ever been named the NFL's Offensive Player of the Year (Although, one of them won the award three times.). Which of the following players never received that honor?

a. Running back Eric Dickerson

b. Running back Todd Gurley

c. Running back Marshall Faulk

d. Running back Steven Jackson

16. Longtime kicker Jeff Wilkins has *missed* more field goals during his Rams career than any other Los Angeles player has even *attempted*.

    a. True
    b. False

17. Who was the Rams' first-ever Super Bowl MVP?

    a. Wide receiver Torry Holt
    b. Running back Marshall Faulk
    c. Quarterback Kurt Warner
    d. Wide receiver Isaac Bruce

18. Which team has defeated the Rams twice in the Super Bowl?

    a. Pittsburgh Steelers
    b. Buffalo Bills
    c. Kansas City Chiefs
    d. New England Patriots

19. In which state have the Rams competed in the most Super Bowls?

    a. Florida
    b. California
    c. Georgia
    d. Louisiana

20. The Rams are undefeated in Super Bowl games that were held within a domed stadium.

    a. True
    b. False

QUIZ ANSWERS

1. D – Quarterback Kurt Warner

2. B – False

3. C – 1999

4. A – 2 on offense, 3 on defense, and 0 on special teams

5. C – Running back Dick Bass in 1966

6. D – A play-by-play radio announcer for the Rams on their home station

7. B – False

8. A – Greg Zuerlein

9. C – Defensive tackle Aaron Donald

10. D – Dallas Cowboys

11. C – 61 yards

12. B – False

13. B – 23

14. A – 1945

15. D – Running back Steven Jackson

16. B – False

17. C – Quarterback Kurt Warner

18. D – New England Patriots

19. C – Georgia

20. B – False

DID YOU KNOW?

1. No Rams have ever won the NFL's Walter Payton Man of the Year Award.

2. London Fletcher began his NFL career in 1998. The linebacker was designated as a Pro Bowl alternate in 11 of his seasons with the Rams, Bills, and Redskins, but did not actually get the chance to play in a Pro Bowl until the 2009 season.

3. Rams icon Marshall Faulk ranks tied for eighth on the all-time list for most rushing touchdowns in the NFL, with exactly 100. Seattle Seahawks great Shaun Alexander is tied with Faulk, and they both sit just 10 scores out of the top five.

4. It is very rare for an entire franchise to be traded, but that happened to the Rams. When owner Robert Irsay bought the team in 1972, he swapped it for the Baltimore Colts with their owner, Carroll Rosenbloom. Rosenbloom continued to own the Rams through his death in 1979.

5. The Rams' value is estimated at $4 billion by *Forbes* magazine, which ranks them as the fourth most valuable NFL team, right between the New York Giants and San Francisco 49ers.

6. Rams linebacker Isiah Robertson was once described by a Pennsylvania newspaper as "the black Dick Butkus" because of his talent and aggression.

7. Los Angeles has a winning record against 15 other current NFL teams. The Rams have gotten the better of the Jaguars, Texans, Jets, Broncos, Falcons, Giants, Buccaneers, Steelers, Chargers, Titans, Browns, Saints, Cardinals, Lions, and Packers.

8. The Rams have played more games against the San Francisco 49ers than any other team in the NFL. The two clubs have faced off 142 times, with no other franchise having more than 93 matchups with the Rams.

9. Rams cornerback Jalen Ramsey once ended up in a brawl on the field with New York Giants wide receiver Golden Tate for entirely personal reasons. Ramsey had been dating Tate's sister Breanna, and Tate was not happy when Ramsey left the relationship after impregnating Breanna.

10. Durability was a cornerstone of Los Angeles linebacker London Fletcher's value. Fletcher played in the NFL from 1998 to 2013 and never missed a game. He started 215 games in a row, setting a record for the linebacker position and leaving him tied for sixth overall among players at any position.

CONCLUSION

There you have it; an amazing collection of Rams trivia, information, and statistics at your fingertips! Regardless of how you fared on the quizzes, we hope that you found this book entertaining, enlightening, and educational.

Ideally, you knew many of these details, but also learned a good deal more about the history of the Los Angeles Rams, their players, coaches, management and some of the quirky stories surrounding the team. If you got a little peek into the colorful details that make being a fan so much more enjoyable, then mission accomplished!

The good news is, the trivia doesn't have to stop there! Spread the word. Challenge your fellow Rams fans to see if they can do any better. Share some of the stories with the next generation to help them become Los Angeles supporters too.

If you are a big enough Rams fan, consider creating your own quiz with some of the details you know that weren't presented here, and then test your friends to see if they can match your knowledge.

The Los Angeles Rams are a storied franchise. They have a long history with multiple periods of success, (and a few that were less than successful). They've had glorious superstars, iconic moments, and hilarious tales. But most of all, they have wonderful, passionate fans. Thank you for being one of them.

Made in the USA
Monee, IL
20 February 2022

91540022R00075